The Let's Talk Library™

Let's Talk About Being a Good Friend

Susan Kent

The Rosen Publishing Group's
PowerKids Press™
New York

To Sally Freeman and Sharon Wolf—two very good friends.

Published in 2000 by The Rosen Publishing Group, Inc.
29 East 21st Street, New York, NY 10010

First Edition

Book design: Erin McKenna

Photo credits and Photo Illustrations: pp.4,8,11,19,20 by Seth Dinnerman; p.7 © Michael Lichter / International Stock; p.12 by Ira Fox; pp.15,16 by Guillermina DeFerrari

Kent, Susan, 1942–
      Let's talk about being a good friend / by Susan Kent.
          p.   cm.— (The let's talk library)
      Includes index.
      Summary: Describes the qualities of a good friend and discusses activities and communication problems involved in friendship.
      ISBN 0-8239-5419-6 (lib. bdg.)
      1. Friendship in children—Juvenile literature.   [1. Friendship.]   I. Title.   II. Title: Let's talk about being a good friend.   III. Series.
      BF723.F68K46 1998
      177'.62—dc21   98-46465
                                                                              CIP
                                                                              AC

Manufactured in the United States of America

Contents

What Is a Good Friend?

A good friend is a person you like and who likes you back. A good friend enjoys doing the things you like to do and is fun to be around. A good friend is someone who is honest and **trustworthy**. Good friends understand how you feel and try not to hurt your feelings. A good friend will be your friend in happy times and in sad times.

Some friendships only last a short time. Other friendships are so special, they last your whole life long.

◀ *Good friends stick together.*

Megan and Steve

Megan's friend, Steve, just got out of the hospital. He was there because he had a broken arm. Megan visits him when he gets home. She brings Steve some presents. He loves the get-well balloon, the toy car, and the books she gives him.

Steve asks Megan to sign his cast. Megan listens while Steve describes how the doctor put his cast on. Then she tells Steve all the news from school. She and Steve have fun spending time together. Megan and Steve are good friends.

Visiting a friend who doesn't feel well shows how much you care about him. ▶

Friendships

There are many different kinds of friendships. The first time you meet someone, you might know she will become a friend. Sometimes you have to know someone for a long time before he becomes your friend. Friends can be your age, or older, or younger. A group of people can be your friends, and you may also have one special friend.

You make friends throughout your whole life. You have friends from when you were little, and friends you have just met. Whether old or new, friendships are important for everyone.

9

Try to meet someone new at school. She might turn out to be a good friend.

Finding Good Friends

It is not hard to find good friends. You can make friends in your neighborhood or at your school. You can meet them at day camp or on the basketball team. You can find them doing things you like to do. They might be in your scout troop or in your dance class.

You might see your friends a lot or maybe not that often. Your good friends might live close by or may be far away. Near or far, good friends are all around you!

These friends study together in class and play basketball after school. ▶

Friends Do Things Together

Friends enjoy doing many things together. They might play sports, ride bicycles, or jump rope. Good friends often talk to each other on the phone. They might go shopping together or watch a movie. Some friends like to do their homework together. Many friends trade baseball cards or stickers with each other. Good friends often like to listen to their favorite music together.

What do you like to do with your friends?

◀ *Being with friends makes everything more fun.*

Michael and Brad

Michael and Brad are best friends. They like to do everything together. They both try out for the Little League team. Brad makes the team, but Michael doesn't. Michael feels left out. He tells Brad how he feels. Brad says he understands. The boys agree they are still best friends, even if they don't always do everything together.

Sharing different **experiences** can be a fun way for friends to tell each other about what they do or where they go when they are not together.

Friends can have fun together even if they're good at different things. ▶

When Friends Don't Get Along

Sometimes even good friends disagree. When you disagree and get angry, you might have an **argument**. It's okay to argue, but you and your friend will need to **compromise**. When you compromise, you both give in a little, and you both get some of what you want. If your friend says something that hurts your feelings, talk about it. Tell your friend how you feel. Be sure to listen, and try to understand what your friend has to say as well. Good friends argue, but then they make up.

◀ *Talking things out helps you stay friends even when you disagree.*

When Friends Change

Sometimes friends change. As you grow older, you might choose to do different things. You might want to play the guitar instead of video games. Your old friends may do things you don't think are fun. You might have trouble finding things to say to each other.

Though it hurts when friendships end, it is important to do what seems right for you. Remember, there are a lot of new people to meet who like the things you do and who can become your friends.

You might feel left out when you don't hang out with your old friends as often as you used to. ▶

Eliza and Casey

Eliza's dog, Boz, is lost. Eliza and her family have searched everywhere, but still can't find him. Eliza is very sad. Casey comes to visit her. Eliza doesn't feel like playing, so Casey just sits with her on her stoop. Even though she is still sad, it makes Eliza feel better to have Casey there with her.

Good friends are there for each other. They offer a shoulder to lean on when things go wrong.

◀ *These girls know they can count on one another.*

You Are a Good Friend

Everyone wants to have friends. In order to have good friends, it is important to know how to be a good friend. Being a good friend is not hard. Here are some things you can do: Be glad for a friend's happiness. **Compliment** a friend who has done something well. Invite a friend to come over and play. Comfort a friend who is sad. Try to help a friend in need.

Being a good friend makes two people happy, you and your friend.

Glossary

argument (AR-gyoo-ment) When people who don't agree about something get angry at each other.

compliment (KOM-plih-ment) Saying something nice about someone.

compromise (KOM-pruh-myz) When people give up part of what they want to come to an agreement.

experiences (ik-SPIR-ee-ent-siz) Events in someone's life.

trustworthy (trust-wur-THEE) To be dependable and honest.

Index